WHAT EVERY MANAGER
SHOULD KNOW ABOUT
SAFEGUARDING CHILDREN

A HANDBOOK

Reg Pengelly

**Grosvenor House
Publishing Limited**

This book is published by
Grosvenor House Publishing Ltd
28-30 High Street, Guildford, Surrey, GU1 3EL.
www.grosvenorhousepublishing.co.uk

A CIP record for this book
is available from the British Library

ISBN 978-1-78148-823-2

Virtual College's Safeguarding Children e-Academy

is proud to sponsor

**What Every Manager Should Know About
Safeguarding Children - A Handbook**

Reg Pengelly was a senior detective officer with Thames Valley Police and completed his service as the Lead Staff Officer for Personal Crime and Forensic Science at the Home Office branch of Her Majesty's Inspectorate of Constabulary. He represented HMIC at the Victoria Climbie Inquiry and led the police team that participated in the first Joint Chief Inspector's national inspection of Safeguarding Children.

On retirement he went on to help write national guidance for the police service on the investigation of child abuse, domestic violence and harrassment. In 2004 he joined the NHS and was subsequently promoted to become the Associate Director responsible for safeguarding across Dorset, Bournemouth and Poole, retiring again in April 2013. He holds a number of management qualifications including a Masters Degree in Business Administration from the Henley Management College.

This short and practical guide has been written for the benefit of managers who are either directly responsible for safeguarding children, or who manage staff whose responsibility includes this, or manage in any organisation that provides services for children. Obvious examples are managers in public sector organisations, head teachers and college principals, leaders of youth and sports organisations, leisure/entertainment providers, faith groups and charities.

Less obvious, are those managers working for the growing number of private sector providers who may be commissioned by public organisations and who by dint of their contractual obligations are under a duty to safeguard and promote the welfare of children.

This book will also be useful to LSCB Chairs as a guide to gauging the quality of safeguarding provided by organisations within their area.

Table of Contents

Introduction

At the outset, I'd like to share some ideas that I think are worth the serious consideration of any manager. Whilst these ideas are my own, they are the outcome of many years of experience in managing safeguarding professionals, often in the context of substantial organisational change.

High profile news stories about child abuse and the way in which an individual or an organisation has failed a child are rarely absent from the national media. Whilst these often prompt useful debates about what should be changed, they rarely if ever highlight the extent to which child abuse occurs in every locality. Regrettably at local levels, a belief persists that child abuse is rare. The fact is that on average, two to four children die every week in the United Kingdom as a consequence of abuse and/or neglect. Many, many more suffer irreversible harm at the hands of those whom society believes are best place to care for them.

Safeguarding children is an activity that takes place in a variety of different settings and at many levels. It is important to note that successful safeguarding is wholly reliant upon individual professionals assuming personal responsibility for taking action whenever they suspect child abuse and following it up in a way appropriate to the circumstances.

More often than not this will involve exchanging information with professionals from other agencies. The critical point here is that your staff ought to feel themselves empowered and supported by their organisation to assume this responsibility. The principal role of managers in this scenario, is to ensure that they are! One of the aims of this book is to provide an insight to managers as to how they can achieve this.

Safeguarding children is a complicated business. It exists within a framework of both criminal as well as civil law. Legislation is supported by a body of statutory guidance, much of which is the outcome of learning from the all too numerous Public Inquiries that have taken place since the second half of the 20th century. To those unfamiliar with the tragic circumstances that led to these Inquiries, some of the guidance can appear to be somewhat draconian. Regrettably it is all too easy to allow the sands of time to erode the solid foundations upon which such guidance was orginally built. Arbitrarily or unwittingly ignoring this guidance on the basis that you think it to be excessive, is quite likely to put a child at risk of continuing harm.

In support of the daily practice of dedicated safeguarding professionals, is a huge and ever expanding catalogue of research and practice guidance. Thus I feel it appropriate at this stage, to provide a warning to all managers who read this. Despite the many years I have worked in this field, I do not know everything there is to know about safeguarding children. In fact there are entire aspects that I have but cursory knowledge of. However at least I know that these aspects exist and I understand how these aspects fit into the overall scheme of safeguarding. It has taken me many years to get to this level of understanding. Any manager who thinks that they can quickly read themselves into this particular portfolio and take unilateral decisions on reconfiguring a service without reference to the expertise of their workforce is making a serious error of judgement. Hopefully, if you have taken the trouble to read thus far, you are unlikely to be one of these managers.

The expertise of safeguarding professionals can easily be routinely ignored or undermined within organisations and even occasionally within the dialogue of Local Safeguarding Children Boards. Expertise in this field is hard won and born out of passion, hard work and dedication. It is a valuable asset and needs to be readily available to all employees who come into contact with children and families in the course of their duties.

Whilst safeguarding professionals rarely have senior management experience, they have much to contribute in terms of assessing the multi-agency impact of any proposed change. Ignoring the important contribution they can make to any relevant proposals is at best a serious blunder and at worst will put children in the way of harm.

Quite rightly, there is a considerable body of legislation and guidance about the protection of personal information. My own experience with health professionals is that they often feel themselves to be in a dilemma when confronted with an apparent concern about a child, owing to the very strict rules about confidentiality that apply to health services. Similarly, my 34 years with the police taught me that much of the activity of response officers is process driven with perceived limited authority to act outside of the process without referrence to senior rank. For most organisations, the potential for substantial fines imposed by the Information Commissioner provide sufficient incentive to stifle communication.

It cannot be emphasised enough that where a concern about a child arises, the welfare of the child ascends above all other considerations, including concerns about disclosing confidential information about the child, their carers or for that matter anyone else implicated in arrangements for keeping the child safe. This overriding principle is reflected in the European Convention on Human Rights as well as the UNICEF Rights of the Child. Where any doubts arise about whether or not to exchange information in child safeguarding, all professionals should feel empowered to take action on the basis of a genuine need to protect. Abuse and neglect is unacceptable regardless of culture, religion, class, ideology and sexuality. Respecting the rights of an adult is never an excuse for failing to protect a child.

Equally important is that in those circumstances that can be justifiably dealt with at a measured pace, advice should be available from a reliable and readily identifiable source. In health services this will be a

Named or Designated Safeguarding Professional, in Children's Services there will be a safeguarding team, in the police service there is a Child Abuse Investigation Team. Any other organisation or agency that does not have an "in house" readily accessible safeguarding expert should be prepared to encourage their staff to contact the local authority Children's Services team for advice whenever they need it.

CHAPTER ONE

A brief explanation of the multi-agency safeguarding environment – process and timing

KEY POINTS

- Safeguarding operates within a legal framework in which key words are carefully defined.
- The welfare of the child is always paramount.
- Children can be determined to be "in need" or at "risk of significant harm" as regulated by local thresholds.
- Strict timescales apply within the child protection process.

Definitions

What is a child?

For the purposes of the legislation covered by this book, a child is someone who has not yet attained the age of 18 years.

Parental Responsibility (PR)

This is defined as all the rights, duties, powers, responsibilities and authority that by law, the parent of a child has in relation to that child. Parental responsibility can be shared by several people. The birth mother, unless the child has been adopted, always has PR. However the birth father may only have PR if married to the birth mother (either before or after the birth) or if since 2003, both parents registered the birth together. Otherwise, there are a variety of Court Orders that may define who has PR, such as Parental Responsibility Orders, Care Orders or Residence Orders.

The important point to note is that PR of a child should always be supported by evidence rather than assumption. Commonly this becomes an issue in circumstances of separation between parents where a father seeks access to a child in the care of a third party (e.g. a hospital or school) or to view the child's records held by a third party.

Competency and Consent

In the context of a variety of circumstances, legislation provides that children may be competent to consent to or participate in certain activities and may at different ages become criminally liable. For example, a child over 16 years may receive health services and will be entitled to confidentiality. In fact in some circumstances where the child is considered to be sufficiently competent to understand the nature and consequences of a treatment, a child <u>under</u> 16 years may consent to receive some services confidentally. This includes sexual health services and contraception.

Managers should ensure that they and their staff have a full understanding of any legislation that sets out the age, competency and consent parameters pertaining to any services that are provided to children.

The law – Children Acts 1989/2004

Much legislation and guidance exists to support the processes for safeguarding children and these are largely concerned with the rather complex relationships between agencies operating in a given local area. The principal legislation can be found in the Children Acts of 1989 and 2004 and the statutory guidance supporting this legislation is provided within *Working Together to Safeguard Children* (as amended in 2013).

The Children Act 1989 places at its core, the importance of working openly and collaboratively with families. Ideally, children are best protected by supporting parents to take good care of their children. Similarly, children themselves have a right to know and should be helped to understand what is going on. Children should be listened to throughout any process that concerns them and their views included in any decisions that are taken.

Section 11 of the Children Act 2004 introduced the legal duty of many public sector organisations, to "safeguard and promote the welfare of children". Discharge of the duty is explained in some detail in *Working Together to Safeguard Children*. Commissioners are also under a duty to "ensure" that anyone that provides a service on their behalf (usually because of a contract), also comply with Section 11 and this should be a matter that is explicitly included in contracts and subject to clear contract governance arrangements.

The legislation and guidance consistently assert sole accountability for arrangements to safeguard and promote the welfare of children upon Chief Executives. Despite this, it is rare for Chief Executives to be held to account; except in the scenario of a Public Inquiry.

In defining what contributes to a child's well being, the Government produced a framework based on five essential outcomes. These are;

Stay Safe
Be Healthy
Make a Positive Contribution
Enjoy and *Achieve*
Achieve economic wellbeing

In the achievement of these outcomes, the development of an integrated multi-professional approach by relevant organisations is considered essential.

The Process for Protecting Children

The following narrative provides a summary of how multi-agency safeguarding happens. Understanding the process will allow managers to determine how their organisation is best placed to respond when a concern about a child arises.

Legislation describes the duties of agencies when;

(i) a child is or may be at risk of significant harm and;

(ii) when a child is in need of support.

There are four categories of abuse. These are;

- Emotional;
- Physical;
- Sexual;
- Neglect.

There are more precise definitions of the categories and these are explained in a variety of documents including in the legislation. In recent years, abuse has been extended to include a child witnessing the abuse of another person, as in the case of a child witness to domestic violence, can be considered to have been emotionally harmed. This rather sensibly means that agendas for addressing domestic violence and abuse should be inextricably linked to those for safeguarding children. More detailed information about this aspect is included later, particularly because domestic violence and abuse is frequently encountered in every strata of society .

The child may as a result of their circumstances, be in need of support. Two levels of need are described in the Children Act 1989. These are "a child in need" and "a child suffering or likely to suffer significant harm". The definition of a "child in need" is very wide. Of critical importance is that a thorough assessment leading to the identification of effective interventions takes place.

Many children "in need" can become "children at risk of significant harm" as a result of a more detailed assessment or because of a deterioration in their circumstances or an escalation of abuse.

There are no objective criteria on which to rely when judging what constitutes significant harm. Under section 31 (10) of the Children Act 2004, the question of whether harm suffered by a child is "significant" relates specifically to the child's health and development. Their health or development should be compared with that which could reasonably be expected of a similar child and the parenting that we would reasonably expect them to receive from their parent/carer.

To understand and identify significant harm, it is necessary to consider:

- the nature of harm, in term of mistreatment or failure to provide adequate care;
- the impact on the child's health and development;
- the child's development within the context of their family and wider environment;
- any special needs, such as a medical condition, communication impairment or disability, that may affect the child's development and care within the family;
- the capacity of parents to adequately meet the child's needs;
- the wider family and environmental context.

Where a child is found to be at risk of significant harm, *Working Together to Safeguard Children* mandates a process for managing the case and this includes the role of agencies that may become involved, and how their involvement should take place. For example, where a crime against a child may have taken place, the police should be informed immediately and they in turn are required to engage within the process so that their investigation is coordinated with activity to safeguard the child.

The Children's Services Authority (often described as "Children's Services") operating at the top tier of Local Government (e.g. a Unitary or County Council), is legally empowered and accountable to act as the central hub for all operational safeguarding activity for children. It is important to keep in mind that the concept of Children's Services as the hub is not simply the legislative position, since all safeguarding activity is coordinated from here but also that it serves a very practical function that is best placed to take the lead in safeguarding activity. It will include a dedicated social work team for "out of hours" advice and support.

In the first instance, all referrals or concerns about a child should be routed to this hub, in line with local arrangements. By this means, the information provided may be viewed in a broader context of knowledge about the child, their family or other circumstances. There is a tiered approach to making assessments of need when such referrals are made, alongside timescales for getting these completed. Where appropriate, strategy discussions take place between the professionals involved and further meetings may take place that may eventually lead to a child protection conference in which a plan for safeguarding the child is agreed, acted upon and monitored.

In very urgent circumstances, the police have powers to remove a child to safety and there is provision for obtaining emergency care arrangements for children from the Courts.

By far the most contentious aspect of the multi-agency safeguarding process is that of so-called "thresholds". There are many facets in determining which cases conclude that a child is in need or at risk of significant harm. Similarly, there are degrees in the level of risk. This is a matter of judgement based on local procedures within the Children's Services team. In some cases referrals will not qualify for the next tier of assessment.

These arrangements amount to what is commonly perceived as a "gatekeeping" exercise, which critics argue is more informed by staff capacity than meeting a child's needs robustly. Staff from other agencies are often extremely frustrated when they feel that this is the case and the outcome in terms of inter-agency relationships has in my experience become corrosive at times. All managers need to be aware of the dangers that thresholds present for relationships between professionals. Inter-agency communication and strong interpersonal relationships are a critical factor in managing this particular risk. LSCBs too, have a role in promoting and supporting such relationships.

For example, many frontline health professionals such as health visitors and school nurses, signal that they are currently managing a much higher level of risk for children in their caseloads than hitherto because cases that might once have been considered to require Social Care intervention are now not reaching that threshold and fall to the referring professional to manage. It is incredibly difficult to measure whether there is any truth to this popular belief, but what is very clear is that nationally, safeguarding caseloads amongst these health professionals have increased significantly. It is equally evident that the number of children that do meet the threshold for child protection plans has also increased and that because of this, the caseloads of Children's Services staff has grown with it.

The Multi-Agency Conference and Timescales

There are strict timescales for activities that support the child protection process. The following is an abbreviated summary taken from the perspective of a referring agency. There are many other functions or options that may be undertaken by Children's Services to support the process.

More often than not, the initial communication that a child is suspected to be at risk of significant harm, is made verbally. Within 48 hours of this initial referral; a formal written report or letter from the referrer must be submitted. This report or written referral form, is often prepared using an agreed multi-agency template made available by Children's Services.

The local authority must decide how to respond to the written report within one working day. This may lead to any one of a number of outcomes. One outcome is that the local authority confirms that the referral amounts to a concern that a child is or may be "at risk of significant harm". This will trigger enquiries pursuant to Section 47 Children Act 1989, giving rise to the expression "a Section 47 case", (meaning that it is a significant harm inquiry).

Where the referral is considered to amount to such a concern, a Strategy Discussion/Meeting between the relevant agencies will take place in which the decision will be confirmed and the next steps to be taken are planned and coordinated.

Where emergency action needs to be taken, for example an urgent care application; such action should normally take place following a strategy discussion involving appropriate agencies. However at any stage where a child might be at immediate risk of significant harm, emergency and sometimes unilateral action may be taken.

Strategy discussions between relevant agencies may take place at any time as appropriate to the progression of the case. These could be formal meetings or telephone calls. However the chair should circulate notes of the meeting to all participants within one working day.

An initial assessment should take place within 10 working days of the date of the referral. This may lead to identification of the child as "in need" and in turn that might lead to preparation of a "core assessment" in which the child's particular needs are explored more fully. A core assessment is a very detailed piece of work that requires careful planning and can take several weeks to complete. The core assessment should in any event be completed within 45 days and agencies have a duty to assist this process by the timely provision of relevant information.

Where the initial assessment confirms the child to be "at risk", a child protection conference must be held within 15 working days of the initial strategy discussion at which the Section 47 enquiries are commenced. It is important that any professionals involved in the case who have a relevant contribution to make and are invited, should attend this conference in person even if they have previously submitted a written report. This invitation is unavoidably, often made at relatively short notice.

All organisations who have staff in respect of whom such short notice invitations may be made, should have robust arrangements in place for resilience or contingency cover that facilitates attendance.

Staff attending the conference will be required to participate in the risk assessment based on their own and other information shared there. If a manager is concerned that an employee may be insufficiently experienced in this part of the conference, they should arrange to attend with them and should make time to talk the case through with the employee beforehand. This aspect also highlights the importance of a sound training experience for staff.

The child protection conference will;

- Share relevant information about the child and family;
- Assess the risk to the child;

- Decide whether the child is at continuing risk of significant harm;
- Decide whether the actions required to safeguard and promote the welfare of the child need to be formulated within the framework of a child protection plan;
- Appoint a key worker who must be a social worker or a nominee from the NSPCC;
- Identify membership of the core group who will develop and implement the plan;
- Ensure a contingency plan is in place if agreed actions are not completed and/or circumstances change;
- Agree about if and when to reconvene and review.

The child, subject to age and understanding may attend the conference and may bring an advocate or supporter with them. Parents and carers are usually encouraged to attend and advised to seek legal advice or an advocate as necessary. This can be intimidating for inexperienced professionals. It will be noted that a core assessment will probably not be completed at this stage. The main decisions of a conference should be shared within one working day although detailed notes of the conference will take much longer to prepare. Individual agencies are expected to keep records of conferences and this includes that in health settings, these should be accessible through health records for the family and child which are normally held by their GP.

An outline child protection plan will be agreed at the initial conference; however a Core Group will be appointed to develop a more detailed child protection plan. The parents are likely to be included in the Core Group as is the child; subject to their age or competency. The focus of the Core Group should be upon the outcomes that will improve things for the child rather than upon the specific actions. The first meeting of the Core Group must take place within 10 working days of the initial child protection conference.

A record is maintained by the Local Authority of all children who are subject to Child Protection Plans. Health Safeguarding Professionals and other health services by local arrangement are able to check whether children are subject to plans (often cited as "on the register", an expression persisting since a time predating the inception of child protection plans). This check will ensure that any information relevant to the continuing safety of the child is passed to the Local Authority.

The first child protection <u>review</u> conference must be held within three months of the initial conference. The review conference requires the same level of commitment as the initial conference and it is essential that relevant professionals attend in person. Except when a child becomes an adult at 18 years, or when the family moves to another area (where responsibility for the plan will be passed to a new team), the Review Conference is the only authority for discontinuing a child protection plan.

From the child's perspective, the outcome of child protection processes might result in a Court determining that they should be subject to temporary fostering arrangements, a stay in a Local Authority care facility or adoption. Children who have not been adopted but remain under the responsibility of the Local Authority by virtue of a Court Order or who in temporary/emergency circumstances are under protection are usually described as "Looked After Children".

Children in these circumstances are extremely vulnerable and often require substantial practical support from a number of agencies. This support needs to be well planned with active participation from the child wherever practicable. A substantial body of guidance has evolved about the role of agencies and this is routinely subject to inspection. Above all, the support to "Looked After Children" should be integrated into the way that each agency delivers services and should not be seen as a specialist role much less something entirely within the remit of a specialist safeguarding service.

The Common Assessment Framework

Assessments of children whose support needs fall short of child protection arrangements, may utilise the "Common Assessment Framework". The CAF as it is more commonly known, helps professionals to identify the most effective support for a family, and facilitates multi-agency collaboration. An assessment can be completed at any time it is believed that a child will not be able to progress towards the five essential outcomes.

The CAF is a four-step process whereby practitioners can identify a child's or young person's needs early, assess those needs holistically, deliver coordinated services and review progress.

STEP 1 - IDENTIFY NEEDS EARLY
STEP 2 - ASSESS THOSE NEEDS
STEP 3 - DELIVER INTEGRATED
SERVICES
STEP 4 - REVIEW PROGRESS

The CAF is designed to be used when a practitioner is worried about how well a child or young person is progressing (e.g. concerns about their health, development, welfare, behaviour, progress in learning or any other aspect of their wellbeing) a child or young person, or their parent/carer, raises a concern with a practitioner, a child's or young person's needs are unclear, or broader than the practitioner's service can address.

The process is entirely voluntary and informed consent is mandatory, so families do not have to engage and if they do they can choose what information they want to share. Children and families should not feel stigmatised by the CAF; indeed they can ask for a CAF to be initiated.

The CAF process is not a "referral" process but a "request for services". The CAF should be offered to children who have additional needs to those being met by universal services. Unless a child is presenting a need, it is unlikely the CAF will be offered. The practitioner assesses needs using the CAF. The CAF is not a risk assessment. If a child or young person reveals they are at risk, the practioner should follow the local safeguarding process immediately.

There can be an unrealistic expectation that a trained Social Worker will always undertake the CAF or will always lead the work to support a child in need or their family. This responsibility will more usually fall to the professional who instigated the original referral, provided they are sufficiently capable.

Since a large proportion of children in need are identified by frontline professionals it is important that operational managers are alert to staff workloads and should ensure that support, supervision and professional advice is provided. I cannot over emphasise the importance of managers maintaining awareness of the implications of this aspect of safeguarding upon the capacity of their staff. A workload of this kind can be overwhelming in terms of personal capacity and their emotional welfare.

Abuse of Disabled Children

Disabled children, being children already "in need", represent a significant number of the total child population and are many times at a higher risk of abuse and neglect. These are children with difficulties that range from physical, sensory and learning disabilities to chronic illness and significant mental health problems.

The principle of "the welfare of the child is paramount" applies in these circumstances more starkly than in most others. The parent/carer's concerns and expectations must never override protection of the child.

The most important action that a manager can take where such chidren may be in the care of their organisation or where services are provided to the child/family, is to recognise the very real risk of abuse and to take steps to mitigate these. Supervision is discussed later in this book and is a very important protective factor in these circumstances. Further guidance on this topic is included in the list of documents at Appendix A.

CHAPTER TWO

The Local Safeguarding Children Board

KEY POINTS

- The LSCB oversees how local agencies safeguard and promote the welfare of children.
- Certain agencies are under a legal duty to engage with the LSCB.
- The LSCB may initiate a Serious Case Review (SCR) into the involvement of agencies where a child has died or is seriously harmed.
- Agencies are expected to respond to the learning from SCR. This may involve fundamental changes to the way they are managed.

Local Safeguarding Children Boards (LSCB) were established as a result of the Children Act 2004. Previously, similar functions were undertaken by bodies known as Area Child Protection Committees (ACPC). It is worth reflecting that many of the arrangements for safeguarding that were included in the 2004 Act arose as a direct result of the Victoria Climbie Inquiry, conducted by Lord Laming. I mention this because the findings of that inquiry demonstrated more than any other, that safe-guarding children should be everyone's business and not just that of the children's social care team. Establishment of LSCBs within a legal framework of partnership was a major advance. Many public sector organisations are under a statutory duty to cooperate with LSCB by virtue of the Children Act 2004.

LSCBs have a legal responsibility to oversee multi-agency safeguarding arrangements and to hold partner agencies (i.e. those under a duty to cooperate) to account for their contribution to those arrangements. Agencies under a legal duty to cooperate with the LSCB include the police, health services, relevant local authorities, departments such as Children's Services, education, housing, and Probation Services and all of these should be represented on the Board by senior (executive) level managers. Other organisations may be invited to take part in the Board and often they will include representatives from the voluntary sector, local armed services and lay members representing the community.

It is usual for LSCBs to take responsibility for organising or at least promoting local safeguarding training, the development of joint policies and protocols, as well as assuring the quality of work undertaken through audits and reviews. LSCBs also have specific legal duties in the organisation of Serious Case Reviews and the Child Death Review process.

Funding for LSCBs is likely to be drawn through contributions made by the partner agencies although there is no legal compulsion for them to do so and there is no central funding provided either. In recent times, LSCBs have appointed independent Chairs to their Boards and most if not all of these, receive a modest salary for their services. This salary is also funded through partner contributions, if not by the Local Authority.

There are many variations on a theme in the way that LSCBs function and often this will be influenced by the personal style of the independent chair. Ideally, the LSCB will have the means to monitor how well or otherwise safeguarding activity is conducted within its area and will set out a clear plan for the year's activities in terms of promoting safeguarding and will monitor progress at Board meetings. In addition, all LSCBs will have the means to quality assure their local safeguarding arrangements.

The work of the LSCB is invariably distributed between a number of sub groups and each LSCB will have their own way of doing things. Of the manifold functions undertaken by LSCBs, two are legal requirements. These concern the establishment of Serious Case Reviews (or Audits) and a process for reviewing all child deaths.

Serious Case Reviews and Audits

There remains room for considerable debate about the effectiveness of Serious Case Reviews as a vehicle for improvement. These reviews are essentially investigations into the reasons for a failure of local arrangements that has led to the death of or serious injury to a child. Until recently, they have followed a highly prescriptive process that was rather bureaucratically followed by an evaluation overseen by Ofsted.

Many critics have claimed that the process became more important than the outcome of such reviews and cite that in many areas, consecutive reviews have found the same mistakes being made time and time again with no signs of learning having resulted in improvement. A substantial review of safeguarding conducted by Professor Eileen Munroe has fuelled the debate further and in turn has led to exploration of alternative approaches to the concept of learning from past mistakes.

Even given new approaches towards less bureaucratic serious case reviews, they remain extremely expensive undertakings, with the services of an independent author/ Panel Chair often costing in the region of £10k. These costs are borne within the LSCB budget but will inevitably be reclaimed through partner agencies. Additionally there will be opportunity cost to organisations undertaking Individual Management Reviews (IMR) and incurred through providing staff to support the conduct of the LSCB Panel that oversees activity. Given the labour and expense of such undertakings, it is wasteful and depressing to find that learning is not always translated into improvement.

Traditionally, Serious Case Reviews and where appropriate, Serious Case Audits have comprised of two components; individual management review reports and a final composite overview report. The individual management report is the report of a review that has been conducted internally within a single agency and the overview report brings together the findings of all composite IMRs and in this context attempts to make sense of any inter-agency activity that has taken place.

More recently a third kind of report has been introduced called the Health Overview Report. This acknowledges the complex inter-relationships between different health providers such as Hospitals, General Practitioners, Dentists etc, bringing together the health service IMRs in support of the subsequent delivery of the Overview Report. It is usual that this report will be prepared by the Designated Nurse covering the health area associated with the LSCB.

The structure and content of both kinds of report has up until recently been required to fit a prescribed format but is now much less regimented. However both types of report require the construction of a chronology of significant events, careful reconstruction of relevant facts and analysis of the quality of practice revealed by reference to research and professional standards. Managers required to undertake IMR should be experienced in the field of safeguarding so that they are best placed to identify critical issues in the chronology and can apply relevant standards and research to their findings.

The intention of these reviews is to facilitate learning so that any mistakes are not repeated. The reviews are explicitly not intended as disciplinary investigations, although it should be acknowledged that from time to time, serious breaches of professional conduct are discovered and this will lead to a separate but parallel investigation.

Her Majesty's Government has made an absolute requirement upon LSCBs to publish the full report of a Serious Case Review. The only exception (in the opinion of LSCB Chairs), is where publication might in itself harm a child. At the time of writing, very few LSCBs have actually published reports and this has led to considerable frustration on the part of the Government, leading to the very real possibility of further legislation.

The most important aspect of these reviews is how any learning from them is translated into improvements and it has to be said that this aspect provides the greatest challenge. Hitherto, there have been two kinds of improvement planning; action plans arising from IMR that pertain to the single agency that conducted them and actions arising from the overview report that affect multiple agencies and the way that the safeguarding process straddles different services. Very often these have migrated into so called "SMART" action plans in which the outcome intended by the IMR or Overview author can and often has been subverted in favour of drafting actions that are measureable.

Of course many actions lend themselves to the SMART approach and these will have the potential to be managed effectively to fruition. Regrettably some of the most important actions from SCR are not so easily addressed. This is because the particular issue that requires improvement is so deeply rooted in organisational culture, processes and practice that without significant internal commitment to change from the organisation concerned, the improvement will simply not happen.

Investigating the root causes of such failures starts in a frank discussion with practitioners. Typical examples of such a scenario are when practitioner capacity is an issue. An overworked practitioner may well as a matter of survival, opt for compromise rather than the most effective intervention. Here, the real culprit is likely to be one or a combination of factors including insupportive organisational structures, a lack of manager oversight, mistrust or less than robust supervision. Change required at this scale will affect the core business of the agency concerned and is clearly well outside the ambit of a process driven SMART action plan.

Different approaches to reviewing cases are currently being trialled as a result of Professor Munroe's findings. Early indications of these are very positive, however the implementation of improvement will remain a challenge to LSCBs and member organisations. An even greater challenge is for organisations, both those participating in LSCBs and others that provide services for children and families, to proactively improve their safeguarding so that the potential for these mistakes is limited from the outset.

A synopsis of the findings from all SCR in England and Wales is published every two years. Here again, as reflected in these national Biennial Reviews, many mistakes are continually repeated with little or no sign of a commitment to improve things. Actually these reviews often highlight the significance of prevention rather than cure.

Biennial Reviews have repeatedly identified;

- Neglect is a background factor in the majority of cases for children of all ages;
- Recently there is a reducing number of subject children on CP Plans;
- Confirmation of the importance of universal services including schools;
- The primary years present the best opportunities for prevention;
- A need for more understanding of risks associated with parental separation;
- Confirmation of the importance of supervision.

The inescapable truth is that the very process of taking change forward can easily subvert the prospects for improvement because;

- SMART recommendations have led to proliferation of tasks that do not always lead to a change in professional behaviour or interaction;
- The type of recommendations which are easiest to translate into actions may not be the ones that foster safe reflective practice;
- Action plans that are easiest to implement address superficial aspects – deeper and wider issues get sidelined;
- Action on recommendations often and incorrectly implies that learning has taken place.

A useful approach to understanding the nature of the problems presented by Serious Case Reviews is presented by Grint (2005) and Ritell and Webber (1973). These are described as of three types;

Critical – requires immediate intervention, needs an answer. Requires use of hierarchical power.

Tame – encountered regularly, so make use of organisational procedures. Requires use of legitimate power.

Wicked – The problem is ill-structured, with an evolving set of interlocking issues and constraints. There are so many factors and conditions, all embedded in a dynamic social context, that no two wicked problems are alike, and the solutions to them will always be custom designed and fitted. There may be no solutions, or there may be a host of potential solutions and another host that are never even thought of.

The nature of wicked problems is such that without a supporting infrastructure that is fit to facilitate implementation, these become too hard to do. Often they are very difficult to "shoehorn" into SMART actions without subverting outcomes. In this context it is very easy to see how they generate barriers.

The reasons why this occurs are complex and worth exploring. The following is a list of barriers that subvert individual initiative. Some elements of this list are equally applicable to the issues that beset the implementation of solutions to "wicked" problems. The list is not intended to be exhaustive;

- Myths and previous experience e.g. that a case may not meet a threshold and therefore is not worth pursuing;
- Myths about information sharing e.g. that it's unlawful;
- Confused language e.g. technical language is interpreted differently by different disciplines;
- Incomplete understanding of the wider family context e.g. issues affecting the capacity to parent;
- Waiting for an acute incident to occur;
- Only dealing with the "here and now", not compiling information and seeing the big picture;
- Lack of professional curiosity;
- Not knowing the person you are dealing with from another agency;
- The collateral impact of reorganisations;
- Personal anxiety and capacity and perceived absence of support;
- Professional helplessness;
- Organisational constraints and lack of resources;
- A natural tendency to want to keep problems tame;
- A fear of complicating already complex dynamics.

Inherent in many of these barriers are personal attributes that amount to people being risk averse and also indicate defensiveness. Arguably these are the results of how individuals are shaped by their working environment and can be a reflection of the organisational culture in which they operate.

An important conclusion is that fundamentally, there is no flaw in the process of undertaking serious case reviews or their potential to identify areas for improvement. So called "systems" approaches are likely to further improve the way that reviews identify problems and desired outcomes/solutions. However, the real challenge lies in the mechanisms for making these solutions happen and especially in circumstances where the problem to be resolved is identified as "wicked".

Some thinking about the outcomes of a culture in which wicked problems could be solved is worthwhile here and this suggests that such a culture might be characterised by professionals who;

- Were being listened to;
- Felt confident;
- Participated in collaborative decisions;
- Were empowered to take ownership;
- Were encouraged to take ownership;
- Had the capacity to take ownership;
- Were supported by their organisation when they took ownership;
- Followed things through;
- Were recognised to be competent.

It would be easy to dismiss much of this were it not for the single inescapable fact that despite our very best efforts, time and time again, our SCRs both locally and nationally identify the same mistakes being made that resulted in serious harm to a child. The principal outcome of this realisation is recognition that SMART action plans are not sufficient in themselves to achieve outcomes that require more than a process change i.e. "wicked" problems. Repeatedly, action plans prompt process change by way of quick wins and the really important outcomes are subverted as a result. No amount of tinkering with the nature of action planning is likely on its own to address this.

It is suggested that an environmental change needs to take place. Professionals need to be empowered to take responsibility and work together so that "wicked" problems can be embraced and resolved. This work needs to be owned throughout the structure and mandated and encouraged through the LSCB. All member organisations need to support the culture change necessary for this to happen. All staff need to know that colleagues from all agencies are being encouraged to work in this way and have the support of senior and strategic management.

One approach to achieving this objective would involve a change to Local Safeguarding Children Board business planning to ensure that the concept of improvement through collaboration with other agencies is embedded throughout organisations and owned at strategic level. However, this cannot happen unless there is agreement from all agencies to adapt their respective organisational infrastructures. This may mean that success is measured differently and goal setting and appraisal processes may also need to change. It is essential to maintain central control as work must be focussed; however, this central control should not just concentrate on easy to quantify processes. There is a wealth of skills and experience in Local Safeguarding Children Boards that can contribute to this development. It is surprising to find that something like this has not already been tried.

Child Death Reviews

Working Together to Safeguard Children provides the statutory framework for processes in relation to reviewing childhood deaths. The LSCB Regulations require LSCBs to establish procedures both to respond rapidly to individual unexpected childhood deaths and to review all childhood deaths in a systematic way. All childhood deaths are subject to local review, usually led by a senior paediatrician. They are then subject to the scrutiny of a local Child Death Overview Panel (CDOP). The core responsibilities of the Child Death Overview Panel are as follows:

(a) To collect and analyse information about each death with a view to identifying;

- any case giving rise to the need for a Serious Case Review;
- any matters of concern affecting the welfare of children in the area of the authority; and
- any wider public health or safety concerns arising from a particular death or from a pattern of deaths in that area.

(b) To put into place procedures for ensuring that there is a co-ordinated response by the authority, their Board partners and other relevant persons to an unexpected death.

From these activities there are a large number of responsibilities that fall to the CDOP and the LSCB to which it is subsumed. Supporting these processes are a number of nationally developed forms that underpin both local activity and the collection of national data about childhood deaths. Given that childhood deaths are mercifully small in number, this also means that at a local level, numbers are usually too few to develop the evidence from which much, if any worthwhile preventative activity could be justified.

However, this also means that any emerging trends or spikes in the data, should trigger closer scrutiny. Feedback about the experience of families is also a useful yardstick that may inform the development of improvements to services. This latter point is especially important when considering the needs of recently bereaved parents. Any deficiencies should become a matter of continuing scrutiny for both the CDOP and the LSCB until they are resolved.

Quality Assurance Functions of LSCBs

The LSCB should provide local oversight of the way that children are safeguarded. This is not simply oversight of the child protection system but should include other aspects that affect the welfare of children too. This is not to suggest that the LSCB should duplicate the work of other bodies; such as for example any local Children's Trust arrangements or the work of the Health and Wellbeing Boards. But the LSCB should be certain that these bodies are indeed holding local agencies to account in respect of the panoply of aspects that affect children's welfare and are able to confirm that there are no gaps in provision.

One important aspect of LSCB oversight should be an audit of all relevant organisations in terms of their discharge of the statutory duty to safeguard and promote the welfare of children under S11 Chidren Act 2004. There are a number of ways to achieve this and many LSCBs already conduct such an audit every year.

LSCBs may also develop a local data collection so that the Board may routinely monitor aspects of safeguarding that it believes will provide a perspective on how well welfare and safeguarding are being conducted. This data at one level is likely to include information about the number of children who are subject to child protection plans, the number of Section 47 referrals received from each agency and the number of children taken into care. At another level the data may show a richer perspective such as (in the domain of children and domestic abuse), how many children are to be found in Domestic Violence Refuges, how long they have to wait to be placed in school and how long they wait to be rehoused. Not much if any of this however, tells the LSCB about the child's experience. The really effective LSCBs will have the wherewithal to obtain feedback directly from children and families about their experiences.

It is likely that all LSCBs will have a sub group or committee responsible for quality assurance functions. Sometimes this responsibility may be divided between two or more groups depending on the type of assurance required. For example, LSCBs should ensure that the recommendations of Serious Case Reviews are followed up and this particular function may fall to a Serious Case Review Panel. Above and beyond that function, the

LSCB may have a group responsible for routine audits of performance which may be thematic or in the form of sampling exercises or perhaps a combination of the two. Such audits may be in the form of file reading exercises or may take the form of a local review meeting in which a number of cases are taken together with the relevant practitioners. For the reasons previously discussed, the rationale is that there is learning from all of this, and most importantly that the learning drives improvement.

CHAPTER THREE

What should be in place in
any responsible organisation;
How to comply with Section 11
Children Act 2004.

KEY POINTS

- Certain public sector organisations and those they commission for services are under a legal duty to comply with Section 11. However those that are not under such a duty are well advised to comply anyway.
- A transparent trail of accountability, with routine monitoring for safeguarding children throughout the organisation is the basic building block.
- Listening to children and taking their concerns into consideration is vital.
- Every organisation should have clear, accessible and well publicised policies for safeguarding as well as domestic violence. Associated guidance demonstrates how children will be safeguarded.

For those agencies whose job it is to protect children and vulnerable people, the harsh reality is that if a sufficiently devious person is determined to seek out opportunities to work their evil, no one can guarantee that they will be stopped. Our task is to make it as difficult as possible for them to succeed. (Bichard Inquiry Report 2004)

Safeguarding and promoting the welfare of children is defined in Working Together to Safeguard Children as;

- protecting children from maltreatment;
- preventing impairment of children's health or development;
- ensuring that children grow up in circumstances consistent with the provision of safe and effective care; and
- taking action to enable all children to have the best outcomes.

Safeguarding children should be everyone's business, regardless of any legal obligations. Every organisation that provides services for children and families or that encounters children and families in the course of its operations, should as a matter of good practice apply the principles of Section 11. If for no other reason, the consequences for any organisation getting it wrong in terms of the safety of a child could be catastrophic. It is thus a matter of risk management for the organisation as well as a moral duty to protect children. Section 11 provides a useful framework that is applicable to all organisations.

However certain public organisations are explicitly under the statutory duty to safeguard and to promote the welfare of children. They are also required to ensure that any providers from whom they commission services, also safeguard and promote the welfare of children. Effectively this will amount to a contractual obligation on the part of any commissioned provider and the public organisation responsible for commissioning should actively monitor the quality of safeguarding within the operation of the contract. This means that public bodies cannot subcontract work to avoid their responsibility under the statutory duty to safeguard and in turn, contractors have the same duty as the public body but this will be a contractual, rather than a legal duty.

For those Local Authorities responsible for Children's Services, the duty under Section 11 is in addition to a large number of other statutory responsibilities and duties pertaining to children and education. Specifically, Section 11 applies to;

- District Councils;
- NHS bodies such as the National NHS Commissioning Board, Clinical Commissioning Groups and Hospital Trusts;
- The Police;
- Probation and Prison Services;
- Youth Offending Teams;
- Secure Training Centres and
- Connexions;
- State Schools and Further Education institutions.

Inexplicable ommisions from this list (even though they are subject to other external inspections and practice guidance/standards) are;

- GP Practices and other Primary Healthcare providers;
- Armed Services (given that children often reside within the relatively closed community of a garrison/base and that young people under 18 years can enlist);
- Independent Schools.

There are a range of other organisations for whom safeguarding is a legal responsibility, but under different legislation. These include;

- Independent Schools and colleges (not just those offering accomodation);
- Early Years Providers;
- Children and Family Court Advisory and Support Service (CAFCASS);
- The UK Border Agency.

Inevitably there are a great number of commercial and voluntary sector organisations that are neither explicitly subject to Section 11 nor under a contractual obligations as a provider, but nevertheless have contact with children and families. Media organisations, broadcasting companies would be included here but remembering that a child includes anyone under the age of 18 years, the list also extends to employers such as manufacturers, distributors, retailers, sports providers, clubs and associations. Taking a responsible approach to safeguarding children should be considered a duty by all of these.

What should be in place

The duty to safeguard and promote the welfare of children requires not just a broad commitment to keep safeguarding in mind in all of an organisation's undertakings; It also requires an infrastructure. The following is a summary of the requirements that appeared in the original statutory guidance to complying with Section 11 and is what could be considered to amount to a Code of Practice that all organisations should measure themselves against. At the very least, it provides a useful checklist;

1. Clear priorities for safeguarding and promoting the welfare of children that are explicitly stated in key policy documents and in commissioning strategies.

There should be clear linkage to safeguarding in any published organisational policy and priority documents so that the importance of safeguarding children is explicit and so that all staff understand that it is a cross cutting priority. This may seem rather draconian at first sight, however many years of experience have demonstrated that unless safeguarding is lodged firmly in an organisations conciousness it rapidly becomes a marginalised aspiration...until things go wrong!

2. A clear commitment by senior management to the importance of safeguarding and promoting the welfare of children through both commissioning and the provision of services by the organisation.

The only person who is truly accountable when safeguarding of a child goes wrong is the Chief Executive.

It is true that to date, this accountability has not translated into a single Chief Executive being sacked. However
it is only a matter of time before an aggrieved child or
parent brings a lawsuit against an organisation, citing
their failure to comply with Section 11 or indeed, that
the Chief Executive of a public body is prosecuted for
malfeasance. If this were not sufficient incentive, the fact
is that without a demonstrated commitment from senior
managers running through the organisation from top to
bottom, there is a significant chance that in turn the
commitment of staff will rapidly erode.

3. A culture of listening to and engaging in dialogue
    with children; seeking their views in ways appropri-
    ate to their age and understanding and taking
    account of those both in individual decisions and
    the establishment or development and improvement
    of services.

Of all the requirements in the guidance, this is one of the
most important and probably the most difficult to
accomplish. Regrettably there is not much of practical
benefit that has been published in the way of supplementary guidance to help organisations to accomplish effective and truly representative engagement with children.
This is frustrating because engagement with children and
young people is clearly the right thing to do, is more
likely to identify practical ways to deliver a service and
to highlight any risks. This means that organisations
need to identify WHICH children they need to engage
with and HOW to accomplish this. It is patently ineffec-
tive merely to challenge a panel of volunteer children if
they do not belong to the target group for services.

A common example of how this has gone wrong is where consultation with a school debating society about the provision of teenage pregnancy services was attempted; none of the children in the group were parents or pregnant. This isn't just about configuring services either; children should be consulted whenever a new role is created that affects them and there is a growing and commendable trend to include a panel of children as part of relevant recruitment processes. In my view, the key to success in this regard is the appointment of a dedicated coordinator whose role may be to solely support the organisation or, one shared between several, according to capacity. Such a role should be intrinsic to corporate communications not simply lodged within safeguarding as it potentially performs a marketing and publicity role too.

4. A clear line of accountability and governance within and across organisations for the commissioning and provision of services designed to safeguard and promote the welfare of children and young people.

All organisations from the smallest to the largest, have a form of governance. It may not be called governance in all of them. What this looks like internally, is a line of accountability through the organisation to Board level. There should be regular reporting and challenge to safeguarding arrangements and one member of the Board should have reporting responsibility. The Board should be clear about what it wants to know so that this is not simply a "rubber stamp" exercise. Similarly if the local organisation is part of a national or perhaps international body, then accountability and governance needs to be explicit throughout. The LSCB will also want to be included in some elements of intra organisational governance and this should be made clear through LSCB meetings and in contracts with providers.

5. Recruitment and human resources management procedures and commissioning processes, including contractual arrangements, that take account of the need to safeguard and promote the welfare of children and young people, including arrangements for appropriate staff checks on new staff and volunteers and the adoption of best practice in the recruitment of new staff and volunteers.

Recent statistics about registered sex offenders in England and Wales demonstrate a ratio of around 81 per 100k of the population. This ratio only represents those who have been caught and succesfully prosecuted; both of which functions are considerable achievements in themselves. None of us really want to admit that this horrendous perversion of human nature exists in our proximity but regrettably it really does exist everywhere and managers of organisations that recruit people who may be allowed access to children should understand and take this very real risk extremely seriously.

Mitigating such risks is not straightforward. Undertaking Criminal Records Bureau (CRB) checks is not enough on its own and in fact it is no longer possible to undertake such a check in respect of people whose only role will be in maintaining records. In any event, many paedophiles, possibly the majority, have escaped succesful prosecution.

Safer recruitment will be discussed in more detail in the next Chapter.

6. A clear understanding of how to work together to help keep children and young people safe online by being adequately equipped to understand, identify and mitigate the risks of new technology.

This aspect on the face of things, applies only in respect of any Internet or other electronic communication access afforded to children by virtue of the service that is provided by the organisation. Possibly the most useful approach to adopt, if this aspect is applicable to your organisation is utilisation of the self review tool provided at www.onlinecompass.org.uk/

Note that many providers including residential homes, hostels and hospitals "outsource" from third parties for the provision of Internet services, often as part of a package, including television. In many such arrangements, the third party establishes a direct contract with the service user. In such circumstances, the organisation that "outsources" the provision of these services is required to ensure that the contractor has taken steps to safeguard and promote the welfare of children who may access these services. This is a really good example of the aspect of promoting welfare, in that access to age-inappropriate material, particularly of a sexual or very violent nature, should be restricted as part of the requirement. Outsourcing therefore is not a way to mitigate risks to the organisation, actually it may well create more risks and certainly requires additional effort in terms of governance.

Consideration should also be given to the potential for professionals employed by the organisation to become drawn into inappropriate communication with children and this especially includes the inept use of social networking. Staff should be provided with sufficient skills to manage privacy and to avoid compromising communications. These aspects are covered later, in the context of the organisation's duty as an employer.

7. There are policies for safeguarding and promoting the welfare of children, including a child protection policy, effective complaints procedures and these are consistent with locally agreed inter-agency procedures as well as any other specific guidance from the Local Authority.

Every organisation that provides services for children and families or that comes into contact with children and families in the ordinary course of business should have a written safeguarding policy and supporting guidance notes for how the policy should be applied, that is readily accessible to all staff. The most cursory search of the Internet will provide many examples of such policies and examples of guidance.

Most, if not all LSCBs have published a huge catalogue of local procedures that are based upon but often enlarge upon the guidance provided in *Working Together*. Not surprisingly, these will be biased around the particular local nuances of service provision that exist in their local areas and so it is really important that the policies of any organisation in such a locality are in accord.

8. There are arrangements to work effectively with other organisations to safeguard and promote the welfare of children, including arrangements for sharing information;

It may well seem from my earlier briefing about how the process of safeguarding children works, that exchanging information is intrinsic to the process and should, by dint of the statutory framework in which it operates, be effective. Unfortunately the process relies entirely upon;

- The knowledge and experience of those who are involved;
- That everyone who comes into contact with children and families understands that safeguarding children is their business and not somebody elses;
- That they know what to do when they have a concern;
- That they know who to contact when they need advice;
- That they know how to make a referral;
- Ideally, they should know who it is they are speaking to;
- They are supported by their managers.

Accountability, authority to act and a sound basis of knowledge are therefore important factors. But just as important is routine dialogue with partners at every level. This in most instances amounts to effective networking between partners, a shared appreciation of each others roles and problems and a culture of mutual support. Great examples are of regular shared lunchtime meetings between GP Practice Staff and the local Children's Service (Social Work) Team, shared local training events such as "managing allegations" training, local conference/training events for domestic abuse etc. LSCBs are well placed to facilitate much of this.

9. Procedures for dealing with allegations of abuse against members of staff and volunteers (note this includes any allegation that suggests a member of staff or volunteer may be unsuitable to work with children for any reason), or for commissioners, contractual arrangements with providers that ensure that such procedures are in place.

A review of internal discplinary arrangements will establish whether these are sufficiently robust to address issues that may arise affecting the suitablity of staff to work with children. *Working Together* provides a process for managing such circumstances in a transparent way that ensures that the member of staff involved receives appropriate support and protection and that any concerns about their suitablity are properly managed and if necessary referred for inclusion in a list of people barred from working with children. One important aspect of the procedures is to ensure that people who have been the subject of allegations, are not able simply to resign before the outcome of an investigation is reached and thus be at liberty to apply for another job resulting in other children being put at risk.

The requirements on organisations are usually supplemented through local procedures published by LSCBs.

In essence they will require an appropriate senior manager from each organisation being nominated as the Designated Manager. This manager will be the conduit to each Local Authority Designated Officer (LADO) who will determine whether a particular case meets the criteria in *Working Together* and will agree a process for oversight of the case with the Designated Manager. In doing so a number of other agencies, especially the police, will become involved, initially to ensure that any other information about the employee that may help to determine their continued suitablility to work with children, is included. This process has often turned up some disturbing information about people who were previously held in high regard; including undisclosed convictions for serious crime and even false identity.

10. Arrangements to ensure that all staff undertake appropriate training to equip them to carry out their responsibilities effectively and keep this up to date by refresher training at regular intervals; and that all staff, including any temporary staff and volunteers who work with children, are made aware of both the establishment's arrangements and their responsibilities for safeguarding and promoting the welfare of children.

At the most basic level, this means that any staff who come into contact with children, no matter in what context, should be at least alert to the possibility of abuse and should know who in their own organisation, they should speak to if they have a concern. All staff should be familiar with the contents of "What To Do If

You're Worried a Child Is being Abused". This national publication can be downloaded at;

https://www.education.gov.uk/publications/standard/publicationDetail/Page1/DFES-04319-2006

However those staff who actually work with children, should always maintain training at a higher level and unless the organisation already has a prescribed level of training agreed through a national professional body such as the Royal College of Nurses, then advice should be sought from the LSCB. This will help to determine the most appropriate level of training, where this can be obtained and the frequency of refresher training. Additionally, a number of private sector organisations offer e-learning for staff and these include a suite of highly regarded products from the Safeguarding Children e-Academy. www.safeguardingchildrenea.co.uk/

11. There are appropriate whistle blowing procedures and a culture is fostered that enables issues about safeguarding and promoting the welfare of children to be addressed.

Historically, the first indication of children being abused in institutional settings has been when a member of staff has reported their collegues. Often in such cases they have been disbelieved by their managers or the seriousness of what was alleged has been played down. Recent revelations about Jimmy Savile indicate that senior managers in the BBC were probably alerted to concerns by their staff and these too were dismissed.

At the heart of such concerns is the very real possibility that a child is being harmed with nobody taking action to protect them. The member of staff who has made the allegation has taken a huge risk in doing so and will be in need of support themselves. Whistle blowing should be taken as a sign of a healthy organisation and every organisation should have a clear policy that all managers are conversant with and actively support.

CHAPTER FOUR

Duties as an Employer

KEY POINTS

- Your staff are a valuable asset. Their selection, management and welfare will inevitably impact on the quality of their work, the safety of children and the reputation of the organisation.
- Safer staff recruitment requires careful management and meticulous attention to detail so that inappropriate individuals do not gain access to children or the records of vulnerable families.
- Legal sanctions exist where organisations recruit staff who are barred, to work with children.
- Where there are any doubts as to the suitablity of an employee to work with children, this should be referred for the advice of a Local Authority Designated Officer and local procedures followed.
- Domestic violence affects children as well as employees. Organisations should be clear about what managers are expected to do when it is disclosed and especially how any children are protected.

Recruiting Staff

All organisations employ staff. The recruitment process as well as the quality of the employment contract are critical in both ensuring that the organisation employs the best people it can find and that they are clear about the organisation's expectations of them. It is a regrettable fact however that becoming an employee of certain organisations is an extremely attractive proposition for some of the most dangerous individuals in society.

In 2012, the NSPCC obtained figures under the Freedom of Information Act, which showed there are 29,837 registered sex offenders who have committed crimes against children (i.e. paedophiles), out of a total of 61,397 in England and Wales. Registered sex offenders are those actually convicted of a crime that is notoriously difficult to prove, especially when the only witness to the crime may be a child. In reality, this means that there are a great deal more paedophiles amongst the population than any official statistics can demonstrate. An important study (Sullivan and Beech, 2004), of so called "professional perpetrators" revealed that;

- 15% chose their career solely to facilitate opportunities to abuse children;
- 41.5% said that abuse was part of their motivation for a particular choice of career;
- 77.5% had arranged meetings with children outside of work hours for the sole purpose of abusing;
- 41.9% had established a reputation at work of being "touchy" or "pervy".

These are uncomfortable statistics and we all want them not to be true. However all responsible organisations should take these facts into account and need to take considerable care when recruiting staff who may have contact with children and their families. This much should I hope, be obvious.

However, arguably less obvious in the context of recruitment is the proliferation of paedophile networks in which information as well as images are routinely exchanged, often in return for substantial payment. This means that access to children is not the only aspect of a particular employment that may be attractive to paedophiles and those who profit from supporting their activities.

By far the majority of children and families that attract the interest of paedophiles are those already vulnerable by dint of a variety of reasons, not the least of which are poverty, ignorance and low self-esteem. There is a strong trade in information about these families between paedophiles through a number of networking opportunities including some that take place in prison, and this is a major cause of children becoming victims of a succession of abuse by different men. Information of this kind is pure gold and the most devious will target organisations for their information about vulnerable familes, not just to groom children through workplace contact.

The propensity of paedophiles to target vulnerable families is therefore a significant consideration. Vulnerable in this context means that they are poor and likely to be not well educated. Above all they exist in a cocoon of dependency in which they instinctively respond positively to anyone apparently in authority and who seems to be on their side. Thus they are highly susceptible to grooming and inevitably, the least likely to be believed in the event of any harm being discovered to their children. If an organisation holds records about such familes, that information is of considerable value and a substantial incentive for employment to both men and women.

The Law

The Safeguarding Vulnerable Groups Act 2006 established the Independent Safeguarding Authority (ISA) to make decisions about individuals who should be barred from working with children and to maintain a list of these individuals. The Protection of Freedoms Act 2012 merged the ISA with the Criminal Records Bureau (CRB) to form a single, new, non-departmental public body called the Disclosure and Barring Service (DBS).

Under the Safeguarding Vulnerable Groups Act 2006 it is an offence for an employer to knowingly employ someone in a regulated position if they are barred from doing so. It is also an offence for the individual who has been barred to apply for a regulated position (one which involves spending regular time working with children).

The Protection of Freedoms Act 2012 reduced the scope of "regulated activity" by focusing on whether the work is unsupervised (in which case it counts as "regulated activity") or supervised (in which case, organisations can request an enhanced criminal records check, but this will not include a check of the barred list). The new definition of regulated activity relating to children comprises of:

(i) Unsupervised activities: e.g. teach, train, instruct, care for or supervise children, or provide advice/ guidance on well-being, or drive a vehicle only for children;

(ii) Work for a limited range of establishments ("specified places"), with opportunity for contact: for example, schools, children's homes, childcare premises. This does not include work by supervised volunteers;

Work under (i) or (ii) is regulated activity only if done regularly. The Government will provide statutory guidance about supervision of activity which would be regulated activity if unsupervised such as;

(iii) Relevant personal care, for example washing or dressing; or health care by or supervised by a professional;

(iv) Registered childminding and foster-carers.

The new definition of regulated activity came into force on 10 September 2012 and was issued in conjunction with guidance on the level of supervision required to take work out of the scope of regulated activity.

Organisations that want to request DBS checks on candidates must either:

• register with the DBS (this is only suitable for large organisations that need to carry out at least 100 checks a year);

- or use an umbrella body that is registered with the DBS (the NSPCC is not an umbrella body). You can search for Umbrella Bodies on the Home Office website.

It is not possible for individuals to request a DBS check either on themselves or on anyone else.

Depending on the nature of the work, an employer may ask for a Standard or an Enhanced Disclosure.

Anyone working in "regulated activity" with children should undergo an Enhanced Disclosure with a check against the barred lists, i.e. adults barred from working with children. Regulated activity includes unsupervised activities which involve regularly caring for, training, teaching, instructing, supervising, providing advice/guidance on well-being, or driving a vehicle for children under 18; or working for a limited range of "specified places" with opportunity for unsupervised contact with children. The definitions for regulated activity are set out in the Safeguarding Vulnerable Groups Act 2006, as amended by the Protection of Freedoms Act 2012.

Enhanced disclosures should also be requested for any position where an individual has regular contact with children. However for positions outside the scope of regulated activity it is not possible to check against barred lists.

An Enhanced Disclosure will give details of convictions, cautions, reprimands and warnings held in England and Wales on the Police National Computer as well as any locally held police force information if it is "reasonably believed to be relevant", by Chief Police Officer(s), to the job role. Most of the relevant convictions in Scotland and Northern Ireland may also be included. It indicates whether the applicant is on the DBS's list of adults barred from working with children (if this has been requested).

Disclosures may not be requested for people under 16 years (for example, school children on work experience placements).

Everyone requesting DBS checks must comply with the DBS's Code of Practice to ensure that the information disclosed will be used fairly. The code also seeks to ensure that sensitive personal information is handled and stored appropriately and is kept for only as long as necessary. Disclosure checks should be stored securely and destroyed after six months.

From the information disclosed by the DBS, the organisation must decide whether the individual is suitable for the position being offered. If the information suggests that an individual might pose a risk to children, then the employer must undertake a detailed risk assessment before deciding whether to appoint them.

At the present time, organisations cannot accept DBS checks undertaken for previous roles in other organisations. This is because, new information may be known about an individual since the last check or different information may be disclosed due to the different nature of the new post.

The Disclosure and Barring Service plans to launch an Update Service on 17 June 2013 which will allow criminal records checks to be re-used for volunteers and employees when they apply for new jobs.

From the 17 June 2013 the DBS will only issue disclosures to the applicant. Employers will need to ask the applicant to see their DBS certificate. If an individual has not shown a new certificate to their employers within 28 days of its issue, the employer may be able to request a copy from the DBS. You can read more about changes being made to the DBS in June on the Gov.uk website.

At the outset it should be made clear that the Disclosure and Barring Service is just one, albeit important tool and should not be relied upon as the sole determination of an employee's suitablity to work with children. In particular, staff whose sole responsibility involves access to records, are no longer eligible for a DBS check anyway as this is not "regulated activity".

At the core of any strategy to mitigate the potential of an organisation unwittingly employing such an individual, are the techniques of safer recruitment. The following should not be taken as a verbatim account of a recruitment process; that is the business of your HR professionals. The following is offered as a specific guide to many additional aspects that are likely to restrict the potential for unwitting employment of a dangerous individual.

Note the point that any organisation that knowingly allows a barred person to work in regulated activity will be breaking the law.

The Safeguarding Vulnerable Groups Act 2006 also imposed the legal requirement on employers to refer to the

ISA (now DBS) information about employees or volunteers who (may) have harmed children while working for them. If you dismiss or remove someone from regulated activity (or you would have done had they not already left) because they harmed or posed a risk of harm to vulnerable groups including children, you are legally required to forward information about that person to the DBS. It is a criminal offence not to do so. If you believe that the person has committed a criminal offence, you are strongly advised to pass the information to the police.

Safer Recruitment

There are four stages of safer recruitment. These should be supported by a Human Resources specialist at every stage. The following is a summary and is not to be taken as an exhaustive description of the process. It should however be sufficient for managers in any organisation to recognise that recruitment in this particular context will require careful reference to the guidance provided by HM Government and referenced in the appendix at the end of this publication;

The invitation to apply

Shortlisting

References & enquiries

Interview

The invitation to apply

This should be considered as an opportunity for deterrence. The job advert should contain a clear message about the organisation's commitment to safeguarding. Any requirement for a DBS check should be made clear at the outset. Formal application forms should be used in preference to CVs. The application form should require the applicant to advise of any unspent or relevant criminal convictions and should also point out a contractual obligation to advise on any criminal investigations current or that occur during the period of employment. Failure to do so should amount to Gross Misconduct. This section should amount to a signed declaration by the applicant. The application form should include;

- A date of birth (to assist in verifying identity);
- Details of current employment and the reason for leaving;
- A full history since leaving school to include all employments, further education, voluntary work etc. This should show all dates of starting and leaving so that any gaps in the record can be explored.
- Qualifications and awarding body as these will need to be verified
- At least two referees (who will be willing to speak with the prospective employer) including their contact details. If the applicant has previously worked with children, one of the references must be from that employer as well;
- A personal statement from the applicant that sets out how they meet the person specification for the job;

- A signed declaration that all of the information in the application is true. Note that it is a serious criminal offence under the Theft Act 1968 to dishonestly make a false declaration in an application for employment.

Shortlisting

This is a crucial time provided to carefully scrutinise the application. Ideally it should involve two people. Care should be taken to identify any inconsistencies and to ensure that the application is fully completed and any evidence provided relates to the person specification and job description. If the candidate is to be selected for interview, highlight any gaps, inconsistencies and concerns so as to ensure that these are explored fully if appropriate through subsequent enquiries/references and always at interview.

References/Enquiries

Ideally, all referees should be spoken to either before any interview or if the applicant has reasonably asked this to be delayed until the outcome of the process is clear; soon afterwards. At the very least, the current/last employer and if the current employment didn't involve contact with children, any previous employer where the applicant did so. With the benefit of the Internet, telephone directories and any other networks at your disposal it should be straightforward to firstly check (i.e. before actually making contact), that the reference provided by the applicant is a genuine manager from a genuine organisation. When contact is made, you should go through the personal information supplied to ensure that the applicant and the person you will be talking about are indeed one and the same. You should always go through the referees statement with them and clarify any ambiguities.

Ask the following questions of the referee and make a record of their responses;

- Whether the referee is aware of any behaviour that might give rise to any concern;
- Whether there were any allegations specifically in terms of the applicants behaviour towards children;
- Whether they were subject to any disciplinary action;
- Confirm the duties and responsibilities of the post they held and the dates of their employment;
- Always fully explore any inconsistencies/ambiguities with the referee.

Of perhaps greater importance than any reliance upon checks is the maintainance of a safe culture within the workplace that ensures that all staff are aware of what they should do when they think a child may be being abused and feel empowered to report their misgivings to someone senior who will take them seriously.

Interviews

All organisations that provide services to children should actively engage with children so that the child's perspective is included in the development of those services. This is a serious commitment and includes having children involved in the recruitment process. Many organisations have already built arrangements for children to be engaged in their recruitment processes and it is truly shameful that many, especially public bodies, have not. This is not about tokenism. Children appropriately engaged in a recruitment process can offer a unique perspective on the qualities of an applicant that can positively enhance the process. This includes shortlisting.

Serious consideration should be given to the use of "screening interviews". The purpose of such an interview is to explore many sensitive personal issues in order to ensure a candidates suitability to work with children. The screening interview should always involve at least two interviewers. The interview should be used; (i) to ensure that the candidate has a full understanding of the job requirements and challenges and (ii) to explore how the candidates life experience has enabled them to develop necessary qualities, skills and aptitudes for the job. The process of conducting the screening interview should include an exploration of any gaps in the employment record and especially any vagueness, a probe of the candidates attitudes towards children and their motivation for working with children and to probe for any prejudices and discrimination.

The applicant should bring originals of their birth certificate or passport and at least two utility bills showing their address. If a passport is not produced, a driving license or other form of photographic identity should be made available. Do not be afraid to seek further documentation if there is any doubt as to the validity of evidence to prove that the applicant is indeed the person they claim to be. You should also ask to see originals of qualifications, professional registration and other relevant documents. Above all, be curious and never accept anything at face value. It is extremely easy using desktop publishing to falsify any amount of very professional looking documents.

Specific arrangements for managing allegations against people who work with children.

Since the tragic events that took place in Soham, a procedure has been developed to manage the circumstances in which an allegation is made or a concern arises that suggests that an employee may not be suitable to work with children. The procedure has been necessary to ensure that where such a concern arises it is used as a trigger for close cooperation between agencies so that any additional information held by others is factored into the inquiry and to provide multi-agency assurance that children are not put at risk by dint of the employee continuing to have inappropriate access to children in that or any other future employment.

Note that this procedure does not just cover circumstances in which the professional has actually harmed a child, it may include those in which ignorance, incompetance, their conduct or their prejudice affects the way that the professional behaves and in doing so may present a risk to a particular child or other children they may come into contact with. Specifically, the procedure covers cases in which it is alleged that a person who works with children has;

• Behaved in a way that has harmed a child, or may have harmed a child;

- Possibly committed a criminal offence against or related to a child; or
- Behaved towards a child or children in a way that indicates s/he is unsuitable to work with children.

It should be noted at the outset that this procedure is applied in addition to any internal diciplinary procedures operated by the employing organisation. Therefore there may be up to three strands in consideration of such an allegation;

- A police investigation of a possible criminal offence;
- Enquiries and assessment by children's social care about whether a child is in need of protection or services; and
- Consideration by an employer as to disciplinary issues.

In this particular context the term employer is used to cover any organisation that has a working relationship with the individual against whom the allegation is made. This includes organisations that use the services of volunteers, or people who are self-employed. Where an employment agency may be involved, both the parties to any contract are deemed to be employers and will need to cooperate in the progress of dealing with the allegation.

The local Children's Services are required to appoint a "Local Authority Designated Officer" (LADO) who is responsible for recording and coordinating progress of the allegation. To that end, the LADO will be available to offer advice to any organisation that raises a concern about a particular individual. Very often the LADO may discern at an early stage that the procedure is not warranted in the circumstances. This will be after the LADO has ensured that nothing else is known about the employee by other relevant agencies. However it is the absolute duty of organisations to report all concerns to the LADO in the first instance and not to "second guess".

Every LSCB member organisation is required to appoint a senior manager (the designated liaison officer) whose role is to manage the interface between their organisation and the LADO. They should also have a nominated "deputy" to act in absentia. For a host of practical reasons it is best that such a manager is directly linked to internal processes for managing complaints or disciplinary procedures affecting employees. This ensures that the line of internal communication is not unduly protracted. It is unlikely that safeguarding professionals would be well placed within their organisations to fulfill such a role, although should be consulted when their specialist expertise is likely to be useful. Most, if not all LSCBs offer training for Designated Managers and this training also offers the opportunity to meet with the respective LADO.

It should be understood that the procedure ensures that the progress of any allegation of this kind is properly monitored by the LADO and;

- that arrangements for the safety of any children involved are confirmed to be in place;
- that no so called "compromise agreements" are reached in which for example, the employee is

allowed to resign in lieu of the allegation being properly tested;

- that the person subject to the allegation is properly supported;

- that where appropriate, any parents of a child/children directly affected by the allegation are kept informed.

The Procedure

If an allegation is made to the police, the officer who receives it should report it to the Force designated (manager) liaison officer without delay and in turn the designated liaison officer should inform the LADO straight away. If the allegation is made to Children's Services, the person who receives it should inform the LADO without delay. All other organisations that receive such an allegation or concern should inform their Designated Manager immediately, who in turn should make contact with the LADO within one working day.

The LADO will obtain full particulars of the allegation from the employer and consider the weight of evidence to determine whether it might be false or unfounded. If the allegation is not patently false and there is cause to suspect that a child may be at risk of significant harm, the LADO will immediately refer to Children's Services to initiate a strategy discussion and the process outlined at Chapter One. Ordinarily such a discussion will include the LADO and employer's representative. If there is no cause to suspect significant harm but there is the possibility of a criminal offence, a similar discussion should be initiated involving the police and again a representative of the employer should be present.

Where initial evaluation does not involve the possibility of a criminal offence, the investigation will be dealt with by the employer. If the nature of the allegation does not require formal disciplinary action, appropriate action must be instituted within three working days. If a disciplinary hearing is required and can be held without further investigation, this should take place within 15 working days.

Where further investigation is required to inform consideration of disciplinary action, the employer should discuss who will undertake this with the LADO. In some circumstances it may be necessary to appoint an independent investigator. In any case the investigating officer should report to the employer within 10 working days. On receipt of the investigation report, the employer should within two working days, decide whether a disciplinary hearing is required If a hearing is required, this should take place within 15 working days. When considering whether a hearing is required, the employer should take into account any relevant information arising from the Children's Services enquiries to deterimine whether the child is in need of protection. There should be routine and effective communication between the LADO and the Designated Manager throughout.

At the conclusion of any investigation, the LADO will be required to consider whether referral to a relevant professional body or the Disclosure and Barring Service is appropriate. If so, such a referral must be made within one month. A referral must always be made if the employer thinks that the individual has harmed a child or poses a risk of harm to children.

For further information about safer recruitment please refer to the DfE Guidance *"Recruiting safely: Safer recruitment guidance helping to keep children and young people safe"*. A web link to this guidance is included in the appendix.

Domestic Violence, your employees and their children

With the benefit of hindsight, it is perhaps astonishing in this enlightened age, to reflect that only up until less than a hundred years ago, it was considered acceptable to for a man to beat his wife. Even within the past 40 years, public authorities were reluctant to take action or to support women who tried to escape such a miserable existence. What is more astounding is that it really didn't make any difference whether there were children associated with whatever horrors were taking place, unless there was explicit evidence that they themselves were being subject to physical harm or neglect.

In recent years, there have been a number of revisions to the definition of what is considered to amount to domestic violence and abuse. You should note that domestic violence itself is not a criminal offence although everything that falls within the definition will amount to a criminal act under various legislation. The utility of the definition is to provide the parameters in which a variety of professionals and policy makers operate. The latest definition, introduced in 2012 is;

Any incident or pattern of incidents of controlling, coercive or threatening behaviour, violence or abuse between those aged 16 or over who are or have been intimate partners or family members regardless of gender or sexuality. This can encompass, but is not limited to, the following types of abuse:

- Psychological.
- Physical.
- Sexual.
- Financial.
- Emotional.

Controlling behaviour is: "a range of acts designed to make a person subordinate and/or dependent by isolating them from sources of support, exploiting their resources and capacities for personal gain, depriving them of the means needed for independence, resistance and escape and regulating their everyday behaviour".

Coercive behaviour is: "an act or a pattern of acts of assault, threats, humiliation and intimidation or other abuse that is used to harm, punish, or frighten their victim".

Note that this definition, which is not a legal definition, includes so called "honour" based violence, female genital mutilation (FGM) and forced marriage, and is clear that victims are not confined to one gender or ethnic group.

Recognition of the plight of children associated with domestic abuse has resulted in a significant change in legislation so that the emotional suffering of children in such circumstances is now recognised as a form of child abuse and this in turn may lead to "child in need" or "at signicant risk of harm" processes.

The British Medical Association estimates that in 75–90% of incidents of domestic violence, children are in the same or next room. Research arising from initial child protection conferences, has found evidence of domestic violence in about half of all cases. Conservative estimates indicate that 30% of children living with domestic violence are themselves subject to physical abuse.

For managers of organisations whose staff may come into contact with women who are or have been subject to domestic abuse, there should be a policy covering how staff should respond with associated guidance setting out what is expected of them. Even if staff do not come into contact with victims of domestic abuse, there should be a policy with associated guidance for managers that covers how the organisation would respond where staff themselves may be subject to abuse. In this regard, particular consideration should be given to circumstances in which both members of a relationship work for the same organisation and also how access to a staff victim might be restricted to prevent a perpetrator abusing them in the workplace. Above all the organisation should have the welfare of any children associated with the abuse as a priority.

MARAC

Multi-Agency Risk Assessment Conferences (MARACs) are meetings where information about high-risk domestic abuse victims (those at risk of murder or serious harm) is shared between local agencies. By bringing all agencies together at a MARAC, a risk focused, coordinated safety plan can be drawn up to support the victim. Over 260 MARACs are operating across England, Wales and Northern Ireland managing over 55,000 cases a year. Surprisingly, these are not legal entities and cooperation with MARACs is a Government expectation but not a mandatory one. It is important to recognise that the MARAC is focused upon developing a safety plan for the victim, not their children. If any children are at risk of harm, they will be subject to a separate, but in most areas, a coordinated protection plan, following the child protection processes outlined earlier. Thus it will be apparent that organisations holding information about a victim as well as their children, may be requested to provide information to support two separate albeit very important functions. All organisations should be prepared to support a MARAC and it would be best to have an internal policy as to how that should be achieved before receipt of any request rather than become the cause of delay.

Domestic Violence – Issues for Managers to Consider

- Domestic violence and abuse is a significant national issue and it is estimated that one in four women will be victims in their lifetime.
- Men are victims as well as women.
- It is for the individual to recognise that they are a victim of domestic violence and abuse and it should be entirely their own decision as to whether to take action or to seek support, if they have capacity.

- Overriding all other considerations, if any children are suspected to be in need or at risk, staff must comply with the LSCB Inter Agency Child Protection Procedures with a view to making a referral to Local Authority Children's Services and if appropriate, should seek advice from a senior manager.

- The effects of domestic violence can be wide-ranging and people experience it regardless of their social group, gender, age, ethnicity, marital status, disability, sexuality or lifestyle. In particular, domestic violence has significant health implications including serious injury, exacerbation of other medical conditions, stress and mental illness.

- The legal obligations, on any organisation, include the duties within the Human Rights Act 1998 and European Convention on Human Rights to protect life and to protect individuals from inhuman and degrading treatment.

- Appropriate partnership working with criminal justice agencies and other statutory and voluntary sector services is essential. Where relevant, your organisation should facilitate full participation in Multi-Agency Risk Assessment Conference (MARAC) arrangements.

- All employers have a responsibility to provide a safe and healthy working environment for their staff. Domestic violence and abuse can affect an individual's work performance.

- Line managers and colleagues should be aware of signs that may indicate that an employee may be a victim. Posters and information in a variety of formats should be displayed in prominent places throughout the workplace.

- Managers should be able to provide information to ensure an employee seeking help has immediate access to professional assistance. This information will include appropriate aid agencies, the police, local refuges and help lines and specialist organisations.
- Employees should be encouraged to talk to their line manager but it is recognised that they may not wish to do this.
- To allow for an informal approach for advice and guidance, staff should be directed to a named employee who may be a union or other representative.
- Where possible, the victim should have access to help from someone of the same sex, sexual orientation or age as himself or herself. It is also important that the contact and those managers involved have received training.
- It should be remembered that dealing with a colleague who is the victim of domestic violence and abuse might be distressing for employees. They may also need support.
- Any employee who is concerned about a colleague should talk to their line manager in the first instance.
- Special paid leave should be provided for appointments where necessary. Examples of this provision would be for counselling, visits to support agencies, solicitors, court, for re-housing or to alter childcare arrangements. Other requests for paid leave and extended unpaid leave should be considered sympathetically. No records of the specific reasons for such absences should be held on the employee's file.

- Periods of absence, including sickness absence, should not have an adverse impact on the employee's employment record where they arise from domestic violence and abuse.
- Requests for advance of pay should be considered sympathetically as should requests for pay to be flexibly paid across different bank accounts to assist the victim to become financially independent.
- Flexible working arrangements may assist an employee in this situation, and should also be given sympathetic consideration.

Domestic violence and abuse is a serious matter that can lead to criminal convictions. Employees should be aware that conduct outside work might lead to disciplinary action against an employee who is perpetrating domestic violence and abuse because it undermines the organisation's confidence in them and is likely to harm the employer's reputation. Terms and Conditions of Employment should require all employees to conduct themselves in a professional manner at all times and to comply with conditions pertaining to any professional registration. All employees should be required to notify their managers immediately when arrested, charged or convicted of any criminal offence. A conviction for domestic violence and abuse could be considered to have brought the organisation into disrepute.

Situations where both the victim and the alleged perpetrator work for the same organisation, or where a victim of domestic violence needs to access services at a location where the alleged perpetrator is employed, need to be handled particularly sensitively. Ensuring safety for the victim and any relevant colleagues in the workplace may involve the suspension or redeployment of the alleged perpetrator pending a disciplinary investigation.

- Misuse of workplace information and resources to continue abuse, should be deemed to be bringing the company/organisation into disrepute and dealt with as a disciplinary offence.
- Perpetrators should be supported in finding help.
- Information about domestic violence and the organisation's policy should be made available to all employees and service users in a way in which they can understand it.

Appraisals

Safeguarding children should be included as an aspect of staff appraisal. At the most basic level, this should act as a triangulation point to ensure that relevant training is up to date, supervision has been taking place and to identify future training needs. This is also an opportunity to test the outcome of any training received and especially whether any change in practice has resulted.

Welfare and Supervision

For the majority of organisations and especially those involved in providing any service for children, their employees are a substantial and critically important resource. Mention has already been made of the emotional impact that can be incurred through working with children and families. This impact rarely takes place in isolation and is often in the context of dysfunctions within the child's family and any personal anxieties arising from the employee's personal circumstances. Furthermore, it is literally true that no two families are the same; each present their own unique suite of issues that challenge even the most resilient of practitioners.

In health and social care organisations, regular clinical supervision is a standard feature of employment in which a confidential review of cases takes place. This is aimed to identify improvements in practice for the benefit of all. This practice often identifies welfare concerns such as stress and particularly any that might be affecting the quality of engagement with families.

People who are working with children and familes deserve the support of their organisations and this includes routine engagement with their managers and peers in a supportive way that encourages them to disclose anything that might affect the quality of their work.

The Social Care Institute for Excellence emphasises how effective supervision is a key component in staff management, which can lead to the following improvements:

- Greater individual motivation;
- Understanding of how work links into overall objectives;
- More effective time management;
- Ability to plan workload;

- More effective coordination of work;
- Better two-way communication;
- Reduction in conflict/misunderstanding;
- Learning on the job; and
- Reduction in stress levels.

Support and supervision sessions are regular one-to-one meetings where work performance is discussed in a systematic manner. The session takes the form of a semi-structured interview with the emphasis on encouraging dialogue between the manager and the member of staff.

Support and supervision is concerned with monitoring work in hand, reviewing progress against individual work plans, discussing problems, developing solutions, and delegating new tasks and projects. Effective support and supervision should maximise learning on the job and support the individual in a way which is appropriate to their stage of development. The wider process of reviewing overall performance and managing personal and career development are best considered as part of a systematic staff appraisal system, although this is a parallel and complimentary management process.

Effective supervision and support will generally cover four broad areas:

- Review of work;
- Delegation of tasks/projects;
- Priority setting; and
- Training and development review.

It should cover both the regular work of employees and other activities such as attendance at various task groups, networks, etc.

For further reading, I heartily recommend a book by the late Tony Morrision; *Strength to Strength A facilitator's guide to preparing supervisees, students and trainees for supervision. ISBN 978 1 84196 175 0*

CHAPTER FIVE

Management in Context

KEY POINTS

- The first step to identifying what needs to be done is to review arrangements within the organisation against the learning from this book and associated references.
- There should be high level support for the review and it's outcomes, accountability for completion with a realistic timescale for completion.
- Expert advice should be sought from any specialists within the organisation or via the LSCB.
- Completion of the review should trigger a programme of improvements that is supported by and routinely monitored by the Executive Board.

The functions of management have been described as;

- Planning;
- Organising;

- Implementing; and
- Controlling.

None of these functions can take place without a sound understanding of what is in place and what needs to be done. In the context of safeguarding children, a first step to planning what needs to be done, is to consider undertaking the review of what what is currently in place and setting this in the context of what should be. Hopefully, the body of this publication will provide you with a useful insight into what should be in place. However a useful checklist from which to explore further is provided under the headings of;

- Accountability;
- Policy and Procedures;
- Staff Recruitment and Training;

- Record Keeping; and
- Performance Information.

This list is not exhaustive. The content will inevitably vary from one type of organisation to another. It is hoped that the following will at the very least provide a starting point.

Accountability

- Is the line of accountability clear to everyone in the organisation?
- Is it clear that the Chief Executive of the organisation is ultimately accountable?
- Is safeguarding children a matter of routine (at least annual) scrutiny by the Executive Board?
- Does this scrutiny include an analysis of performance information (see below) pertinent to safeguarding activity?
- Is a member of the Board (i.e. at the level of Director or equivalent) personally responsible to the Board for safeguarding operationally?
- Is a senior manager nominated as a Designated Liaison Officer for Managing Allegations?
- Is there a deputy for this role available to act in absentia?

Policy and Pocedures

- Does the organisation have an explicit and accessible policy in place for safeguarding children?
- Is the policy subject to periodic review? By whom?
- Is the policy subject to approval at Board level?

- Does the organisation have a domestic violence and abuse (DVA) policy? (This may be included in other Human Resource policies.)
- Does the DVA policy explicitly discuss the action to be taken where children may be affected?
- Is safeguarding children a matter of routine discussion at workplace meetings, particularly those in which service user concerns are discussed?
- Where a disclosure/suspicion of a safeguarding concern or DVA arises, is this considered in respect to risks presented to other family members?
- Where a child is subject to a child protection plan and is referred to another agency/specialist, are there arrangements to ensure that the other agancy or specialist is made aware of the fact of the CP Plan and the name of the relevant Children's Services worker?
- When a child misses an appointment, this should be followed up.

Staff, Awareness and Training

- Are the principles of safer recruitment included in recruitment processes?
- Is safeguarding training mandatory for specific staff groups?
- Are all staff who may come into contact with children provided awareness training of what to do when they think a child is being abused, on induction or soon afterwards?
- Does the organisation have systems to identify which staff should be trained in safeguarding at a higher level than basic awareness?

- Is the training at any level available in a timely way and accessible for all relevant staff?
- Have the Designated Liaison Officer and Deputy received training in Managing Allegations?
- Is there acceptable compliance with training at any level provided? (Suggested 90% or higher for most organisations.)

Records

- Are personal records of children and their families capable of being "flagged" to allow for identification by appropriate professionals of children at risk of harm or those subject to a CP Plan?
- Can family members be readilly linked across records even though they may not live at the same address?
- Are disclosures of DVA recorded?
- Are all entries timed and do they show the identity of who made them?
- Are any arrangements for record keeping compliant with Data Protection Legislation and any other pertinent rules of confidentiality to the organisation?
- Are all referrals and any other concerns recorded in such a way as to illuminate staff workloads as well as to monitor the timeliness of reports and outcomes?

Performance Information

It is vital that resources are allocated on the basis of evidence rather than instinct. In this regard, safeguarding should not be an exception. This means that information about resources, activity and caseloads should be readily available and capable of interpretation. These should be monitored frequently at the level of line managers and at least monthly at a more senior level. An analysis of the data should be presented to the Board at least annually. Most of the issues subject to the review process outlined above would lend themselves to a variety of useful indicators.

However by far the most challenging aspect of performance is that of measuring staff capacity and the potential for catastrophic overload. There are no tailor-made formulae that can be applied across all organisations or for that matter similar ones. A single member may be able to manage a large number of complex cases in one scenario and another working in a more intensive provision may be overwhelmed by a small number of similar cases. The most important point to be made here is that this is not an area in which to "fly by wire". It should be a priority for managers to determine an acceptable caseload formula based upon the type and nature of cases through consultation with staff and their respective unions/professional bodies. By that means, and only by that means can risks associated with staff overload be properly assessed and managed. It is a salutory fact that in my experience, too few organisations have attempted this seemingly obvious piece of work and as a result seem to rely solely upon staff absenteeism and resignations as the only clue to an impending disaster.

Conclusion

The most important step that any manager can take in establishing a safe organisation is to undertake a review of what is in place against the advice contained in this book. This will provide the necessary evidence to support the kinds of critical changes that will make yours a safe organisation. Above all else, the establishment of high level monitoring that provides a true insight as to the way your organisation safeguards children is of vital importance.

At the most basic level, the list outlined previously in the chapter can be used as the framework for such a review. Ideally, those staff who already have some experience of safeguarding within the organisation should be consulted for their advice as to other relevant issues that should be included.

A further useful source for compiling the content of a review can be obtained from the LSCB. The majority if not all LSCBs conduct periodic audits of member organisations to determine the extent of compliance with Section 11 Children Act 2004. It would be useful to factor such an audit into any internal review not just as an economy of scale but also because it will reflect local circumstances and concerns.

Finally, I'd like to recommend the free weekly email updates about developments in the world of safeguarding children, provided by the NSPCC. The service is called CASPAR. You should note that the database suppporting this facility is searchable. Contact the NSPCC on;

0800 800 5000 or email; help@nspcc.org.uk

Appendix A

Supplementary guidance on particular safeguarding issues; all which can be found on the internet;

Department for Education guidance

Working Together to Safeguard Children (2013);
http://www.education.gov.uk/aboutdfe/statutory/g00213160/working-together-to-safeguard-children

Safeguarding children who may have been trafficked;
https://www.gov.uk/government/publications/safeguarding-children-who-may-have-been-trafficked-practice-guidance

Safeguarding children and young people who may have been affected by gang activity;
https://www.gov.uk/government/publications/safeguarding-children-and-young-people-who-may-be-affected-by-gang-activity

Safeguarding children from female genital mutilation;
http://www.education.gov.uk/childrenandyoungpeople/safeguardingchildren/a0072224/safeguarding-children-from-female-genital-mutilation

Forced marriage;
http://www.education.gov.uk/childrenandyoungpeople/
safeguardingchildren/a0072231/forced-marriage

Safeguarding children from abuse linked to faith or belief;
http://www.education.gov.uk/childrenandyoungpeople/
safeguardingchildren/a00212811/safeguarding-children-
from-abuse-linked-to-faith-or-belief

Use of reasonable force;
http://www.education.gov.uk/aboutdfe/advice/f0077153/
use-of-reasonable-force

Safeguarding children and young people from sexual
exploitation;
http://www.education.gov.uk/childrenandyoungpeople/
safeguardingchildren/a0072233/safeguarding-children-from-
sexual-exploitation

Safeguarding Children in whom illness is fabricated or induced;
https://www.gov.uk/government/publications/safeguarding-
children-in-whom-illness-is-fabricated-or-induced

Preventing and tackling bullying;
http://www.education.gov.uk/aboutdfe/advice/f0076899/
preventing-and-tackling-bullying

Safeguarding children and safer recruitment in education;
http://www.education.gov.uk/aboutdfe/statutory/g00213145/
safeguarding-children-safer-recruitment

Information sharing;
http://www.education.gov.uk/childrenandyoungpeople/
strategy/integratedworking/a0072915/information-sharing

Recruiting safely: Safer recruitment guidance helping to keep
children and young people safe;
http://webarchive.nationalarchives.gov.uk/20130401151715/
https://www.education.gov.uk/publications/eOrdering
Download/safer%20recruitment%20guidance%20-%20
nov%202009.pdf

Safeguarding Disabled Children: Practice guidance;
https://www.gov.uk/government/publications/safeguarding-
disabled-children-practice-guidance

DfE: What to do if you're worried a child is being abused;
https://www.gov.uk/government/uploads/system/uploads/
attachment_data/file/190604/DFES-04320-2006-Child
Abuse.pdf

Department of Health: The Framework for the Assessment of
Children in Need and their Families 2000;
http://webarchive.nationalarchives.gov.uk/20130401151715/
https://www.education.gov.uk/publications/standard/
publicationDetail/Page1/DH-4014430

**Guidance issued by other government departments
and agencies**

Foreign and Commonwealth Office/Home Office: Forced
marriage;
https://www.gov.uk/forced-marriage

Ministry of Justice: Guidance on forced marriage;
http://www.justice.gov.uk/protecting-the-vulnerable/forced-marriage

Home Office: What is domestic violence?
https://www.gov.uk/government/policies/ending-violence-against-women-and-girls-in-the-uk

NHS National Treatment Agency: Guidance on development of Local Protocols between drug and Alcohol Treatment Services and Local Safeguarding and Family Services;
http://www.nta.nhs.uk/uploads/supportinginformation.pdf

Youth Justice Board: Guidance on people who present a risk to children;
http://www.yjb.gov.uk/publications/Resources/Downloads/Offences%20against%20Children%20-%20Guidance.pdf

UK Border Agency: Arrangements to Safeguard and Promote Children's Welfare in UKBA;
http://www.ukba.homeoffice.gov.uk/sitecontent/documents/policyandlaw/legislation/bci-act1/

Home Office: Disclosure and Barring Services;
https://www.gov.uk/government/organisations/disclosure-and-barring-service

Child protection and the Dental Team – an introduction to safeguarding children in dental practice;
http://www.cpdt.org.uk

Ministry of Justice: Multi-Agency Public Protection Arrangements guidance;
http://www.justice.gov.uk/downloads/offenders/mappa/mappa-guidance-2012-part1.pdf

Ministry of Justice: HM Prison Service Public Protection Manual;
http://www.justice.gov.uk/offenders/public-protection-manual

Missing Children and Adults – a cross Government strategy;
https://www.gov.uk/government/uploads/system/uploads/attachment_data/file/117793/missing-persons-strategy.pdf

Department of Health: Recognised, valued and supported: next steps for the Carers Strategy;
https://www.gov.uk/government/publications/recognised-valued-and-supported-next-steps-for-the-carers-strategy

Guidance issued by Non Governmental Organisations

BAAF: Private fostering;
http://www.privatefostering.org.uk/?gclid=CLvorZLL_qcCFUlkfAod9Tsatg

Royal College of Paediatrics and Child Health: Safeguarding Children and Young people: roles and competencies for health care staff – Intercollegiate document, September 2010;
http://www.rcpch.ac.uk/sites/default/files/asset_library/Education%20Department/Safeguarding/Safeguarding%20Children%20and%20Young%20people%202010G.pdf

General Medical Council: Protecting children and young people – The responsibilities of all doctors; http://www.gmc-uk.org/static/documents/content/Child_protection_-_English_0712.pdf

Royal College of Nursing: Looked after children – Knowledge, skills and competences of health care staff (Intercollegiate role framework); https://www.rcn.org.uk/__data/assets/pdf_file/0019/451342/RCN_and_RCPCH_LAC_competences_v1.0_WEB_Final.pdf

NICE: Guidance on when to suspect child maltreatment; http://guidance.nice.org.uk/CG89/

Supplementary guidance to support assessing the needs of children

DfE: Childhood neglect – Improving outcomes for children http://www.education.gov.uk/childrenandyoungpeople/safeguardingchildren/childhoodneglect

Note that a longer list of associated guidance may be found in an appendix to "Working Together to Safeguard Children" (2013). However many of the weblinks provided have become obsolete due to archiving and the transfer of functions between reformed government departments, and locating them will require some research.